Destination Detectives

China

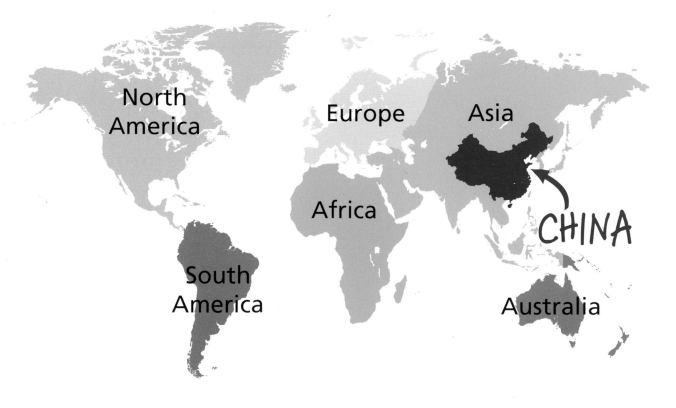

North America

Europe

Asia

Africa

CHINA

South America

Australia

Ali Brownlie Bojang

Raintree

Chicago, Illinois

© 2006 Raintree
a division of Reed Elsevier Inc.
Chicago, Illinois

Customer Service   888–454–2279

Visit our website at www.heinemannraintree.com

Printed in China by South China Printing Company

10 09 08 07 06
10 9 8 7 6 5 4 3 2 1

Library of Congress Cataloging-in-Publication Data
Brownlie Bojang, Ali, 1949-
  China / Ali Brownlie.
    p. cm. -- (Destination detectives)
  Includes bibliographical references and index.
  ISBN-13: 978-1-4109-2331-8 (lib. bdg.)
  ISBN-10: 1-4109-2331-2 (lib. bdg.)
  ISBN-13: 978-1-4109-2342-4 (pbk.)
  ISBN-10: 1-4109-2342-8 (pbk.)
  1. China--Juvenile literature. 2. China--Geography--
Juvenile literature. I. Title. II. Series.
  DS706.B73 2006
  951--dc22
                        2005032916

Acknowledgments
The author and publisher are grateful to the following for
permission to reproduce copyright material:
The Art Archive pp. 17 (William Sewell); Corbis pp. 9
(Reuters), 10 (Keren Su), 13 (Xinhua), 15t (Royal Ontario
Museum), 28 (Ron Watts), 29 (Keren Su), 33 (Chi
Haifeng/Xinhua), 38 (Michael S. Yamashita), 38–39 (Vince
Streano), 42 (Wang Jianmin/Xinhua Photos); Photolibrary
pp. 4–5 (Pacific Stock), 7 (IFA-Bilderteam Gmbh), 10–11
(Panorama Stock Photo), 12 (Panorama Stock Photo), 15b
(Pacific Stock), 19 (Index Stock Imagery), 20–21 (Panorama
Stock Photo), 21 (Panorama Stock Photo), 24 (Panorama
Stock Photo), 27 (Panorama Stock Photo), 31 (Panorama
Stock Photo), 34 (Botanica), 35 (Pacific Stock), 37, 40
(Daniel Cox), 41 (IFA-Bilderteam Gmbh), 43r (Panorama
Stock Photo); TopFoto pp. 16 (Nathan Strange/uppa.co.uk),
23r (Uppa Ltd), 25 (Image Works), 39; WTPix pp. 5t, 5m,
5b, 6, 8, 14, 18, 22, 23l, 26t, 26b, 30, 32, 36, 43l.

Cover photograph of lion dance reproduced with permission
of Panorama Stock Photo Co., Ltd/OSF/Photolibrary.

The paper used to print this book comes from sustainable
resources.

Contents

Some words are shown in bold, **like this**. You can find out what they mean by looking in the glossary. You can also look out for them in the Word Bank box at the bottom of each page.

Where in the World?

The Middle of the World

Zhong Guo is the **Mandarin** word for China. It means "middle or center kingdom." The ancient Chinese people believed that they were at the center of the world and that the Temple of Heaven in Beijing was the center of China.

You are being chased by a dancing dragon spitting fire. Suddenly you hear a loud bang and the dragon runs away. You wake up and realize that you have been dreaming. There is a lot of noise outside. You look out of the hotel window and see children laughing and shouting as they watch firecrackers going off. It's almost midnight. People start to count down: "Four, three, two, one! *Xin nian yu kuai*! Happy New Year!" Fireworks light up the sky.

Lion dances are performed at New Year celebrations. People believe lions ward off demons and bring good luck in the coming year.

WORD BANK Mandarin official language of China

It is the Chinese New Year, and everywhere children are showing off their new clothes and counting the pocket money they have received to mark the occasion. New Year celebrations start sometime between January 30 and February 20 with the new moon and end on the full moon 15 days later. This is a noisy and colorful introduction to your journey around China. Beijing, the capital of China, is your starting point.

Find Out Later...

Where is the world's largest palace?

What was this huge wall built for?

What type of exercise are these people doing?

So This Is China!

China at a Glance

SIZE:
3.7 million square miles (9.59 million square kilometers)

CAPITAL:
Beijing

POPULATION:
1.3 billion

RELIGION:
Confucianism, Buddhism, Taoism (see pages 38 and 39)

OFFICIAL LANGUAGE:
Chinese **Mandarin**

CURRENCY:
Yuan RMB (RMB stands for *renminbi*, which means "people's currency")

TYPE OF GOVERNMENT:
Communist republic (ruled by one political party—the Chinese Communist Party)

You notice a map of China on the wall. You can see that it is a huge, irregular-shaped country. It is only slightly smaller than the United States, and two and a half times the size of Western Europe. Someone has been here before you and stuck labels on the map.

Unusually shaped **limestone** hills are found in the southern **provinces** of Yunnan and Guizhou. This is known as karst scenery.

The Chang Jiang River is 3,987 miles (6,380 kilometers) long—roughly the distance from Seattle to Chicago and back! It is the third-longest river in the world. It runs from the mountains in the west to the East China Sea.

WORD BANK   **autonomous** being separate or able to govern a region independently
limestone rock created from the remains of sea animals

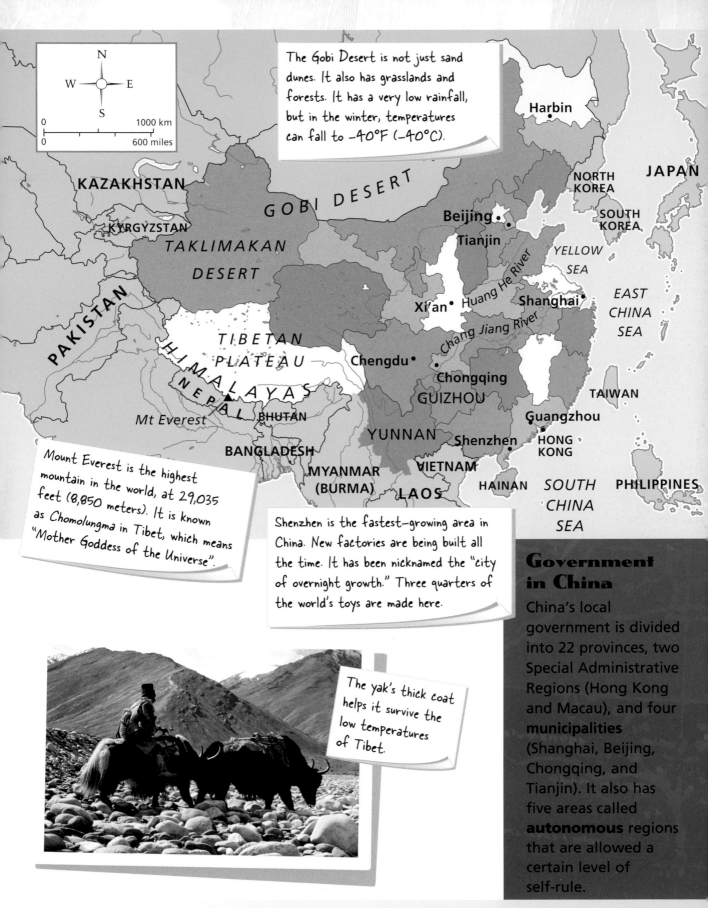

The Gobi Desert is not just sand dunes. It also has grasslands and forests. It has a very low rainfall, but in the winter, temperatures can fall to –40°F (–40°C).

KAZAKHSTAN

KYRGYZSTAN

GOBI DESERT

TAKLIMAKAN DESERT

Harbin

NORTH KOREA

JAPAN

SOUTH KOREA

Beijing

Tianjin

YELLOW SEA

PAKISTAN

TIBETAN PLATEAU

HIMALAYAS

NEPAL

BHUTAN

Mt Everest

Xi'an

Huang He River

Chang Jiang River

Shanghai

EAST CHINA SEA

Chengdu

Chongqing

GUIZHOU

TAIWAN

YUNNAN

Guangzhou

BANGLADESH

Shenzhen

HONG KONG

MYANMAR (BURMA)

VIETNAM

LAOS

HAINAN

SOUTH CHINA SEA

PHILIPPINES

Mount Everest is the highest mountain in the world, at 29,035 feet (8,850 meters). It is known as Chomolungma in Tibet, which means "Mother Goddess of the Universe".

Shenzhen is the fastest-growing area in China. New factories are being built all the time. It has been nicknamed the "city of overnight growth." Three quarters of the world's toys are made here.

The yak's thick coat helps it survive the low temperatures of Tibet.

Government in China

China's local government is divided into 22 provinces, two Special Administrative Regions (Hong Kong and Macau), and four **municipalities** (Shanghai, Beijing, Chongqing, and Tianjin). It also has five areas called **autonomous** regions that are allowed a certain level of self-rule.

municipality main city in China that has the same status as a province
province region that has its own local government

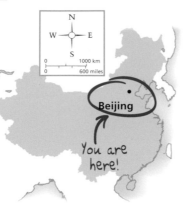
You are here!

The Forbidden City

The Forbidden City is known as *Gu Gong* in Chinese and was for hundreds of years the home of emperors. Building began in 1406, and it was completed 14 years later. It is the world's largest palace, covering 183 acres.

Exploring Beijing

The next morning you wake up early and make your way to the center of Beijing. You find yourself surrounded by buildings and open spaces. Emperors and **peasants** alike have lived and visited here for thousands of years.

You walk across the vast space of Tiananmen Square. This is a popular meeting place for the people of Beijing. Thousands gathered here in 1949 to celebrate the founding of their new country, the People's Republic of China. In 1989, hundreds of students were killed by soldiers while on their way to the square to demonstrate for more freedom from the government's strict laws. Today it is full of young children flying kites and tourists making their way to the Forbidden City.

Tiananmen Square

Tiananmen Square is one of the largest public spaces in the world. At 4.7 million square feet (440,000 square meters), it is big enough to hold half a million people.

The Forbidden City is now one of the most popular tourist attractions in the world.

中华人民共和国万岁   世界人民大团结万岁

WORD BANK   peasant poor person who lived and worked off the land

Desert winds

Looking up at the sky you notice that a yellow cloud has blocked out the sun. A wind is starting to blow and the children are having trouble holding on to their kites. High winds from the Taklimakan Desert in the west are bringing clouds of choking sand to the capital city. People have difficulty breathing and many wear masks. Drivers cannot see where they are going. The government is building a wall of trees north of the city to try to prevent future sandstorms from affecting Beijing.

Olympics 2008

As part of its preparations for the 2008 Olympics, Beijing expanded its airport, developed a high-speed railway, built a new sewage-treatment plant, and improved the city lighting.

Beijing's traffic crawls through a sandstorm. The winds can reach up to 44 miles (70 kilometers) per hour, and the swirling sand makes it difficult to see.

Climate and Landscape

Beijing Winter

In Beijing the climate is hot in summer but cold in winter. When it snows, people come out of their houses with brooms and sweep the snow away from the streets. If you decide to come back here you'll need to bring some warm clothes. The wind blows straight from the coldest place on Earth—Siberia.

China is so huge that the **climate** and scenery change dramatically between different regions. It ranges from bitterly cold in the northern winters to unbearably hot in the southern summers. It has a "north **drought** and south flood" climate pattern. In other words, there is not enough rain in the north and too much in the south.

In the northern city of Harbin, winters are so cold that people are able to build giant sculptures made out of snow.

WORD BANK   drought   temporary shortage of water
dynasty   series of rulers from the same family

In the north the summers are warm—and can be hot—but the winters are very cold. In contrast, the south has a **tropical** climate. Winters are warm and summers are hot and humid. During the summer, **typhoons** often happen and can cause terrible devastation. During these violent storms, winds can reach speeds of 74 miles (120 kilometers) per hour. In September 2005, the most powerful typhoon in 30 years hit southern China, and thousands of people had to be evacuated from villages along the coast.

Temperature Extremes

	Minimum	Maximum
Beijing	-4°F (-20°C)	100°F (38°C)
Turpan	14°F (-10°C)	117°F (47°C)
Lhasa	3°F (-16°C)	84°F (29°C)
Guangzhou	34°F (1°C)	100°F (38°C)

Skiing

The long, cold winters and the mountains in Manchuria (to the north of Beijing) make ideal conditions for skiing. China's largest ski resort, at Yabuli, used to be a royal hunting ground in the Qing **dynasty**. The emperors used to hunt tigers and bears here.

Families enjoy a day out on one of Shenzhen's tropical beaches in southern China.

tropical anything to do with the region on either side of the Equator, the imaginary line around Earth

The Chang Jiang

Chinese people call the Chang Jiang the "Mother River," because its water helps produce the crops that feed the population. In some years, however, it brings floods that can cause much destruction of homes and farmland.

Highlands and lowlands

To the west and the south of China lies the huge Tibetan **Plateau,** which covers more than one-third of the country. This is a very rugged area. It is difficult to live here because of the harsh **terrain** and cold **climate.** Along the plateau's southern edge lie the Himalayas, the highest mountain range in the world.

To the east lie the main lowland **floodplains,** formed by **fertile silt** and soil left by the rivers. China's two main rivers are the Chang Jiang (Yangtze River) and the Huang He (Yellow River). The rivers are important ways of transporting goods between the east and west of the country, especially bulky materials such as coal. These floodplains are China's main farming areas and are where most people live.

On the Tibetan Plateau, movements in the earth have created large rock formations (seen at the bottom here), known as "clay forests."

WORD BANK   floodplain area that floods when river water rises
silt fine particles of sand and rock carried and then deposited by a river

The Three Gorges Dam

A huge dam is being built on the Chang Jiang river, due to be completed in 2009. It will allow ships to travel as far as Chongqing, bringing more business and jobs. The force of the water will be used to power

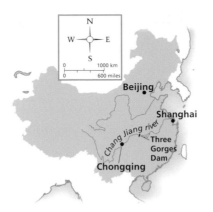

turbines that will produce electricity. The dam will control the river and help stop the terrible flooding that has killed more than one million people in the last 100 years. However, many people are worried that this project will damage the environment and drown towns and villages when the reservoir fills with water. What will happen to all the people who will have to move?

The Dam Project

The Three Gorges Dam will be 606 feet (185 meters) high and 6,500 feet (1,981 meters) wide. The power plant will supply up to 15 percent of China's energy. It will flood and cover 13 cities, 140 towns, 1,340 villages, and 74,130 acres of farmland. About 1.3 million people will have to move from their homes.

◄ When completed, the Three Gorges Dam will be the largest **hydroelectric** dam in the world.

terrain area of land
turbine engine powered by water

A Bit of History

You decide to continue your exploration of Beijing by visiting the Imperial Palace. This is just one of the many museums that show visitors what China was like in the past.

An Inventive Nation

Many inventions have come from China. These include paper and printing, fireworks and **gunpowder**, the wheelbarrow, kites, and the compass. Kites were used in wartime to send messages to prisoners. Some kites were designed to make strange sounds so that they would scare or confuse the enemy.

Chinese dynasties

For thousands of years, the Chinese people—nearly all of them poor **peasants**—were ruled by a series of different families, known as **dynasties**. Each dynasty is remembered for something special. For example, during the Xia dynasty, about 4,000 years ago, writing was invented. During the Qin dynasty, about 200 B.C.E., a series of smaller walls began to be joined together to make the Great Wall of China. This huge wall was meant to keep out attackers from the north, but it was not completed until the 15th century, nearly 1,600 years later.

The Great Wall of China was built out of stone, brick, and earth. It stretches for 3,946 miles (6,350 kilometers) across northern China.

WORD BANK   gunpowder explosive powder used to shoot bullets from guns

The Ming dynasty (1368–1644) is famous for producing beautiful pots and vases. This is why we now call such things "china." The Ming dynasty is also remembered for being very powerful and sometimes very brutal and cruel toward the peasants.

A camel caravan sets out along the Silk Road in the Taklimakan Desert.

These beautiful porcelain vases from the Ming and Qing dynasties are all more than 300 years old. They are worth a great deal of money!

The Silk Road

The Silk Road was a route though deserts and mountains that connected China to the Middle East and Europe. People have been using the Silk Road for more than 2,000 years. People traded goods along the way—from China there was silk, herbal medicines, bamboo, paper, and gunpowder and from the West, gold, grapes, and rugs.

Mao's Little Red Book

Mao was famous for his "Little Red Book," a collection of quotations from his speeches. Millions of copies of it were printed. While Mao was leader, Chinese people were urged to carry it with them at all times.

The Communist republic

By the beginning of the 20th century, many Chinese people were fed up with their rulers, the emperors. The people had put up with many natural disasters such as floods, earthquakes, and famine. They felt that the rulers had done nothing to help them.

In 1934, a man named Mao Zedong, the leader of the **Communists**, led his supporters, known as the Red Army, on a long journey across China to escape from their enemies. This became known as "The Long March," because it took 370 days. Along the way, many more people joined the march. In 1949, Mao became China's leader and the country became a Communist republic. The state took care of its people "from the cradle to the grave," and China had little to do with other countries.

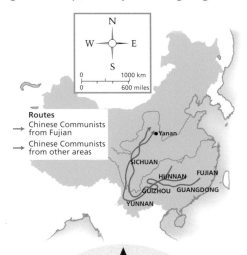

Routes
→ Chinese Communists from Fujian
→ Chinese Communists from other areas

This is a copy of the "Little Red Book." It includes a picture of Mao Zedong.

During "The Long March", Mao and his supporters traveled 4,960 miles (8,000 kilometers) from the south to the north of China.

Communist person who follows a political belief system that calls for a classless society

China changes

After Mao died in 1976, the new leaders decided that China needed to do more business with the rest of the world. Many new factories were built, often with money from foreigners. Goods can now be produced in China cheaper than anywhere else in the world, because people work for low wages. This makes a lot of money for the country. Some people are much better off, but millions are still very poor, especially those working in the factories.

Hu Jintao

In March 2003, Hu Jintao became the President of China and continued the country's **reforms**. He comes from Anhui **Province** and enjoys table tennis and ballroom dancing.

The Four Modernizations

In 1975, Dong Xiaoping, then leader of China, introduced the "Four Modernizations." This was a plan to increase production and **manufacturing**. It was the beginning of the huge changes China has gone through in the last 30 years.

A poster from 1949, showing crowds in Tiananmen Square celebrating the founding of the new Chinese republic.

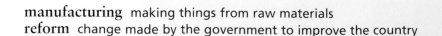

manufacturing making things from raw materials
reform change made by the government to improve the country

Getting Around

Already you are fascinated by China, and you can't wait to begin exploring the different regions. You need to find out how to get around this huge country.

Because China is so big, the quickest way of seeing the different areas is to travel by plane. The national airline, Air China, flies to more than 100 cities. However, flying is an expensive way to travel, and most Chinese people cannot afford it. Many people travel by train or bus instead. Trains and buses are often very crowded, especially during national holidays when everyone is traveling to be with their families. Some long-distance buses show movies to help pass the time.

Rail Travel

The train from Beijing to Hong Kong takes 24 hours. You can choose whether to sit all the way or sleep in a bunk bed. The cabins usually have four beds. A bathroom is shared between all the passengers in the carriage.

The Trans-Siberian Railway

You can go all the way to China from London, UK, or Paris, France, by train. The Trans-Siberian Railway takes nine days and you have to change trains three times.

These buses are hurrying people to work in Kowloon, Hong Kong.

China has an extensive railway network, and more lines are being built, particularly in the southwest.

N W E S
0   1000 km
0   600 miles

Harbin
Shenyang
Alataw
Urumqi
Dalian
Beijing
Shijiazhuaug
Luoyang
Xi'an
Nanjing
Shanghai
Wuhun
Hangzhou
Chengdu
Chongqing
Guilin
Shenzhen
Kumning
Kowloon
Nanning
(HONG KONG)
Sanya

Bikes and cars

All over China, except in the very hilly places such as Chongqing, you can see people getting around on bicycles. It is estimated that there are more than 300 million bicycles in China.

Over the last few years, some people have become richer and have bought their own cars. In large cities such as Beijing and Shanghai, new roads are being built all the time to try to deal with the increasing number of cars.

Underground Trains
Shanghai, Beijing, Hong Kong, Guangzhou, and Tianjin all have their own underground rail system, or subway.

Car Boom
More than 2.2 million cars were sold in China in 2004. This was nearly 14 percent more than in the previous year. People are buying cars in China faster than anywhere else in the world. However, only 3 in every 1,000 Chinese people own a car today.

These cyclists are waiting for the traffic lights to change. Bicycles are an important way of getting around in China's towns and cities.

City Life

You are here!

You decide to go to Shanghai, the largest city in China, to find out more about life in China's **urban** areas. You book a sleeper—a bunk bed on the train—because the trip takes 12 hours and travels through the night. You jump on the train at Beijing station at 7 P.M. and arrive at Shanghai railway station in Puxi at 7 A.M. the following morning.

Booming Shanghai

You make your way to the ferry that will take you to the Pudong area of Shanghai. The boat is crammed with bikes and scooters, and you push your way through to the stall that sells five-spice eggs—spicy scrambled eggs. These are a Chinese specialty, which you buy for your breakfast.

Pudong

Pudong is the new part of Shanghai. Development began on the area in 1990. It is the main trade and financial center and lies on the other side of the Huangpu River from old Shanghai. Bridges, tunnels, and a ferry connect the two areas.

The ultra-modern skyline of Pudong in Shanghai features the Oriental Pearl Tower. It is 1,536 feet (468 meters) high.

For an amazing view of the city, you go to the top of the Oriental Pearl TV Tower. Below you is a city of 13 million people. You can hear the roar of bulldozers and the pounding of jackhammers on hundreds of building sites far below. New hotels, office blocks, and roads are all being built here. Shanghai is typical of how China's cities are rapidly changing.

The Maglev train can take passengers the 19 miles (30 kilometers) from downtown Shanghai to the airport at Pudong in just eight minutes.

Great Heights

The Shanghai World Financial Center will be one of the tallest buildings in the world when it is finished, at 1,614 feet (492 meters).

The Magical Maglev

The Maglev is Shanghai's new **metro** train. It works by using very powerful magnets that lift the entire train 0.4 inch (10 millimeters) above a special track. It has no driver, causes no pollution, and can travel at speeds of up to 311 miles (500 kilometers) per hour.

Shanghai and Beijing have really impressed you. They have shown you some of China's ancient past, as well as how modern and lively Chinese cities can be. So what is it like to live here? You decide to find out how people start their day.

Early-morning exercise

You get up early and take the **metro** to Jing An Park. It is 6 A.M. and already there are lines of people doing slow, controlled exercises and **meditating**. They are doing tai chi, a traditional Chinese form of exercise involving a series of slow body movements.

There are some old men sitting on folding chairs at easels, painting Chinese characters. One of them offers you his brush so you can try it out. Sometimes the artists get up and join in with the exercises.

Rush-hour in Shanghai

By 7:30 A.M. everyone has finished exercising, and the sidewalks are full of people rushing to work or school. Nearly everyone is wearing Western clothes and has a cell phone, usually worn on a strap hanging from their neck. The buses are beginning to fill up. Some people are hailing taxis.

Tai chi is one of the Chinese **martial arts**. It exercises the mind as well as the body.

WORD BANK   martial art type of unarmed self-defense, often practiced as a sport

Calligraphy artists are believed to live long lives.

Calligraphy

Chinese calligraphy dates back thousands of years. People who do calligraphy paint Chinese characters as a way of expressing how they feel and to help them concentrate and relax.

Shopping has become a popular pastime in China's big cities. This is a crowded street in Shanghai.

Leisure time

People in cities have more leisure time now than they used to have. Shopping in the new modern malls, eating out, or going to clubs and discos are popular ways of relaxing. Many people still enjoy the traditional Chinese Opera. These are musical dramas that involve mock fighting and acrobatics. The actors paint their faces and wear colorful costumes. Younger people are more interested in pop singers such as Cui Jian. He plays rock, techno, and hip-hop music to crowds all over the country.

China Online

More than 94 million people in China use the Internet. On average, a Chinese person spends 12.3 hours a week online. More than 20 million regularly play online games in Internet cafés, which can be found everywhere in China—even in hair salons and butchers shops!

This bustling modern indoor shopping mall is in Shanghai.

Hutongs

In most of China's cities, big changes are taking place and many people are benefiting. There are some disadvantages to this fast progress, though. Many old buildings are being torn down to make room for new ones. The *hutongs* of Beijing are old houses built close together around a small courtyard. These are disappearing fast to make room for apartment blocks and wider roads. This means that the traditional close community life, where everyone knows one another, is slowly disappearing.

City Facts

- More than 500 million Chinese people live in cities.
- There are nearly 700 cities in China.
- There are 11 cities in China that have a population of more than two million.
- China's big cities are in the east. There is no city in the west of the country with a population of more than one million.

A gateway leading into an old *hutong* in Beijing.

You have a look in a guidebook to see which other cities in China are worth visiting.

Hong Kong

The United Kingdom took control of Hong Kong from the Chinese after the countries were at war between 1839 and 1842. In 1997, the United Kingdom handed it back. From a small fishing village, it has grown to be the world's fourth-largest banking and financial center.

This is a fish market in Hong Kong.

Seaports

China's 11,250-mile (18,000-kilometer) coastline has been described as the busiest in the world. Most of China's manufactured goods are taken to many different countries by ship from its seaports. The main **ports** are Shanghai, Shenzhen, Hong Kong, Guangzhou, and Tianjin.

Hong Kong is a busy, exciting city, with a mix of traditional Chinese life and modern Western businesses.

Harbin

Harbin is a thriving industrial city in the north. Its buildings look Russian, because many of them were built when Harbin was a stop on the rail journey from Russia.

Guangzhou

Guangzhou is a very old city, dating back nearly 3,000 years. It is now at the heart of a rapidly growing **manufacturing** area.

Xi'an

Xi'an is one of the world's four major ancient cities, along with Athens (Greece), Cairo (Egypt), and Rome (Italy). It lies at the western end of the Silk Road.

Chengdu

Chengdu is believed to be the cleanest city in China. It is famous for its parks and hibiscus flowers. It lies in the middle of some of China's most **fertile** land, and its markets are always full of fresh vegetables and fruits.

The World's Chinatowns

Many cities across the world have their own Chinatown, where you can find Chinese restaurants, shops, and movie theaters. You will find Chinatowns in New York, Chicago, and San Francisco in the United States; London and Manchester in the United Kingdom; and Sydney and Melbourne in Australia.

Chengdu has a population of 10 million and a history dating back 2,300 years.

Life in the Countryside

You are now eager to move on and see more of China. You pack your bag and jump on a bus, leaving the city far behind. You gaze out of the window and see villages and fields rolling by. You notice a man walking behind a plow being pulled by a water buffalo. It is all very different from the hustle and bustle of the city.

Paddy Fields

Growing rice needs a lot of care and a lot of people. The fields—known as paddies—are flooded with water, because rice needs a lot of water to grow. Each plant is sown by hand in the soft soil. The fields need constant weeding before the rice is harvested. Rice farming is backbreaking work.

Farming

Farming is very important in China, because it provides food for the country's huge population. China is **self-sufficient** in food. People and animals do most of the work rather than machines, but every day more and more farmers are using tractors and other machines. This is increasing the amount of food China can produce.

A farmer plows his rice field.

WORD BANK   arable land that is suitable for growing crops
growing season period when it is warm enough for crops to grow

In hilly areas, farmers have learned how to use every bit of land possible to grow their crops. **Terraces** follow the **contours** of the hills, making it possible to grow crops just about anywhere. Some of the terraced fields are more than 700 years old.

In the north there is a short **growing season** and water is in short supply. In the south, the warm **climate** allows farmers to have two or sometimes three crops a year.

Fast Fact

China has 23 percent of the world's population but only 7 percent of the world's **arable** land. Even so, it grows enough food to feed all its people.

Key Crops

China's main crops are rice, wheat, millet, corn, cotton, tobacco, sugarcane, and citrus fruits such as oranges and lemons. In 2004, China had a bumper harvest: 518 million tons of grain—42 million tons more than the previous year.

This woman is weeding rice on a terrace. Terraces are built on steep land to keep soil from being washed away.

self-sufficient able to produce enough food for the population
terrace step or ledge cut into a hillside

Village life

You get off the bus just outside a small village and walk down the wide main street. There are elderly people sitting around a table playing mah jong, a game where you build walls with tiles. Mah jong is popular with people all over China.

Many young people have left the village to find work elsewhere. Most of the families in the village rely on the money these young people send home. About 64 percent of Chinese people still live in the countryside, although this percentage is getting smaller each year, as people leave to find work in the cities. To improve life for people in the countryside, the government is rebuilding old schools and providing electricity and safe drinking water in areas that do not already have these things.

A farmer and his wife take their produce to market.

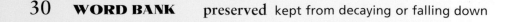

Courtyard homes

You decide to have a look around one of the houses. It stands in a courtyard, where hens peck at the dirt and pigs grunt in the corner. Rice has been scattered at the far end to dry in the sun. The yard is surrounded by houses. The man who lives here is head of the family, so his house faces south and gets the most sunshine—the most favored position— while the other houses are occupied by his grown-up children and his brother's family.

Ancient Architecture

Many villages in China are hundreds of years old. They are now being **preserved** as special examples of Chinese architecture. They have become popular tourist attractions. Some of them have been used for filming movies such as *Crouching Tiger, Hidden Dragon* (2002).

China's Villages

There are more than 700,000 villages in China, most of them based on farming. They are usually small, with about 200 to 500 inhabitants.

桃李争春

喜气盈门家多财心贵

福星高照人平寿级好

Children play around the entrance to a courtyard in a country village.

Inside a courtyard home

Like most of the other houses in the village, this one has electricity, and there is a small black-and-white television. There is no running water, though. The children of the family get water from a nearby well. Life in villages like this has not changed much in the past 100 years.

Inside the house, a table is covered with dishes of rice, noodles, pork, chicken, and vegetables, all grown or raised in the country. The family invites you to join them, and you dig in with your chopsticks.

Village schools

In the villages, children start school when they are six and stay there for nine years. If they want to go to a junior high school, they have to pass an exam.

These boys are on their way to school in rural China.

Chinese children learn subjects similar to those taught in Western schools, but there is one big difference—Chinese children have to learn Chinese characters by heart. This is much more difficult than learning the alphabet.

Many children in **rural** areas leave school early because they need to help their families with the farming.

Chinese characters often look like the words they represent. These are the characters for "rain" and "tree."

Schools in rural areas, like this one, receive less government **funding** than those in the towns and cities.

Schooling in China

Many schools in rural areas lack enough teachers and up-to-date books. They receive less money from the government than schools in the cities. On average 44.3 yuan ($5.50) is spent on primary-school students in cities, but only 28.12 yuan ($3.50) is spent on every rural student.

People and Culture

You have met many people on your travels so far, but there are more than a billion people in China, and there are lots of differences between them.

The people of China

There are 56 different **ethnic groups** in China. Each group has its own language and traditions, although everyone learns **Mandarin** at school. The Han ethnic group is by far the largest, making up about 90 percent of China's people. They are found everywhere in China, but most live in the low-lying areas in the east. The second-largest ethnic group is the Zhuang. There are about 18 million Zhuang in China —nearly as many as the population of Australia!

Shrinking Families

In order to prevent the population from becoming too large, the government encourages most families to have only one child. This does not apply to some minority ethnic groups or people living in **rural** areas, who need children to work on the farms.

China's Main Minority Groups

Ethnic Group	Population
Zhuang	18 million
Manchu	9.8 million
Mongolian	4.8 million
Tibetan	4.6 million

Some Chinese people are only allowed to have one child.

WORD BANK   ethnic group people with the same culture or nationality

Some of the larger ethnic groups live in the border regions in the west and north. The Chinese government has given them more power to rule themselves. For example, the Uighur and the Tibetans have their own **autonomous** regions.

Chinese Customs

- Chinese people do not like to say "no" or to say that they don't understand something. This can be very confusing!

- If someone gives you a present, stand up and accept it with both hands. Do not open it right away.

- When visiting someone, always bring a small gift such as flowers or some chocolates.

Tibetans are one of China's main ethnic groups. These women are wearing traditional Tibetan dress, which is very colorful, with beads and necklaces.

Sports

The Chinese are a sports-loving nation. To find out more about this and Chinese culture, you travel back to Beijing.

Soccer has become hugely popular, and Chinese people follow the teams in the English Premier League. You join some Chinese friends and go watch a game in Worker's Stadium. People shout slogans and wave their red flags as the Chinese side beats the other team. Other popular sports include gymnastics, table tennis, and tennis.

Chinese Sports

China has introduced many sports to the rest of the world, including archery, polo, and wrestling.

Chinese Holidays

The anniversary of the People's Republic of China is celebrated on October 1. In 1999, the government decided to celebrate this national day by giving everyone a one-week holiday. This encouraged people to travel to visit friends and family, as well as tourist attractions.

The Chinese enjoy many different sports. Here, a group of young men play basketball in a city park.

Food

The different regions of China offer a wide variety of foods to choose from. Rice is the main food, although around Beijing and the north people eat more bread and noodles. In Szechwan, people use a lot of hot peppers in their cooking, which can make the food hot enough to burn your mouth unless you are used to it.

Fish is an important part of the diet for many Chinese people. People often eat fish on New Year's Eve, because it is thought to bring wealth and prosperity. There are more than 150 different species of fish in the seas and rivers, including hairtail, chub mackerel, herring, octopus, and squid. Fish are also bred in ponds and lakes inland.

In the cities you can get any kind of food you want, from hamburgers and pizza to duck's feet.

China Tea

Legend has it that tea was discovered when some leaves blew into the Chinese emperor's cup of hot water in 2737 B.C.E. China produces several different kinds of tea including strong gunpowder tea, and the more delicate Lapsang souchong.

A Food-Loving Nation

The Chinese say that they will eat anything that has four legs except a table and anything that flies except an airplane.

This is a steaming wonton —a dumpling filled with seafood, meat, or vegetables.

Religion in China

You have noticed many temples on your travels around China, but there is no official religion here. In fact, the government banned it for a long time. Now, though, people are free to follow their own beliefs.

Many people follow Confucianism. Confucianism is not an organized religion. It is more like a set of rules for living. Confucius lived about 3,000 years ago. He taught that people should love one another, rule without force or violence, and treat others as they themselves would like to be treated. His influence can still be felt today.

Ancestor Worship

Most Chinese people honor and worship their **ancestors**, whatever their religion. People regularly visit their graves and leave them things such as soap. In return, they hope their ancestors will help them get a job or find the right marriage partner.

This is a Buddhist temple in Kunming, in the **province** of Yunnan.

An elderly man lights incense at the graveside of his ancestors as a way of honoring them.

WORD BANK   ancestor person from whom you are descended

Taoism is another important religion in China. Tao means "the way," therefore Tao is the path that people should follow. Buddhism was introduced to China from India more than 2,000 years ago. Millions of people all over China are Buddhists, especially in Tibet. Islam came to China from Central Asia, and today there are about four million Chinese Muslims. **Missionaries** brought Christianity to China in the early 17th century.

The exact numbers of people following different religions in China is not known. Religion was banned for so many years that even now, people do not always like to say that they follow a religion.

Fast Fact
China has more than 13,000 Buddhist temples.

Yin and Yang

Yin and Yang are part of Taoism. Yang is everything in the world that is hot, hard, and masculine and is often represented by the color white. Yin is dark and hidden and feminine and is often represented by the color black. These forces have to be balanced to live in perfect harmony.

The Yin and Yang symbols represent harmony and order in the world. Yin is dark and Yang light.

Wildlife and Environment

Animals

There are more than 2,000 species of **terrestrial vertebrates**, 1,189 species of birds, 500 species of mammals, 210 species of **amphibians,** and more than 320 species of reptiles in China. Mammals include snow leopards, elephants, wild yaks, reindeer, bears, and tigers.

There are only 1,600 pandas left in the wild. About 1,000 more are under protection in zoos and wildlife refuges.

Back in Beijing you decide to visit the zoo. Your favorite animal is the giant panda (*Ailuropoda melanoleuca*), and this is one of the few places you can see one. The giant panda is China's most famous animal. It only eats bamboo. Bamboo trees are being cut down and used for scaffolding for the building industry and to make furniture. This makes it difficult for pandas to continue to live in the wild.

Animals and plants

The variety of different animals and plants in China is among the greatest in the world. Some of the country's most famous animals are threatened with **extinction**. The places in which they live and the food they eat are being destroyed by China's rapid development.

WORD BANK amphibian animal, such as a frog, that lives both in water and on land
extinction no longer existing

Environmental issues

China has serious environmental problems. Forests are being cut down. After all the trees have been cut down, it is easy for water to wash the soil away and for wind to blow it away. This problem is called erosion, and it can cause serious flooding. It also can ruin the land for farming and can create deserts. Burning coal to produce electricity and the rapid increase in the number of cars pollutes the air. The government is planting trees all over China and is introducing more controls to prevent as much pollution as possible.

China's beautiful landscapes are at risk of being ruined by pollution and other environmental problems.

Pollution

China burns coal to produce its energy, and this produces a thick, unhealthy, polluting smog over many cities. Chongqing is nicknamed "Fog City" because of the pollution.

Stay or Go?

You have been very lucky to have this quick glimpse of China, especially at a time when it is changing so quickly. There is still plenty to see and do, so what will you do —stay or go?

Still to see and do

- Shanghai's brand-new Formula One racetrack.
- The huge army of **terra-cotta** warriors that guard the tomb of the country's first emperor, Qin Shihuang. There are more than 10,000 figures and chariots.
- A three-day cruise down the Chang Jiang from Chongqing to Wuhan.
- The caves at Longgong in Guizhou, which extend through 20 mountains.
- The white pagodas and stone forest water festivals and temples of Yunnan **Province**.
- The Grand Canal, built in 495 B.C.E., which links the Huang He and Chang Jiang rivers. It is the longest artificial river in the world.

China in Space

After China's first astronaut came back from space in October 2003, he said he was unable to see the Great Wall of China from space. This is something schoolbooks have claimed for years. China was the third country, after the United States and Russia, to put an astronaut into space.

Yang Liwei, China's first astronaut, steps out of his capsule after his trip into space.

WORD BANK   terra-cotta type of clay

This is the amazing terra-cotta army, near Xi'an.

Thousands of tourists every year now travel through Pudong, one of Shanghai's two international airports.

A Tourist Hotspot

According to the World Tourism Organization, China will be the world's number-one tourist destination by 2020. The government now also allows Chinese tourists to travel to the United Kingdom and Europe. Until recently, only business people could do this.

Find Out More

Destination Detectives can find out more about China by checking out the resources listed on this page.

World Wide Web

If you want to find out more about China, you can search the Internet using keywords such as these:

- China
- Beijing
- Yangtze River

You can also find your own keywords by using headings or words from this book. Try using a search directory such as www.yahooligans.com

More Books to Read

The following books are packed with lots of useful information about China:

Cotterell, Arthur. *Eyewitness: Ancient China*. New York: DK Children, 2005.

Dramer, Kim. *People's Republic of China*. Danbury, Conn.: Children's Press, 1999.

Field, Catherine. *Nations of the World: China*. Chicago: Raintree, 2000.

March, Michael. *Country File: China*. North Mankato, Minn.: Smart Apple Media, 2003.

Morris, Noelle. *World Tour: China*. Chicago: Raintree, 2002.

O'Connor, Jane. *The Emperor's Silent Army: Terracotta Warriors of Ancient China*. New York: Viking Juvenile, 2002.

Movies

Crouching Tiger, Hidden Dragon (2000)
Directed by Ang Lee, the film tells the story of a warrior's search for his stolen magical sword.

Time Line

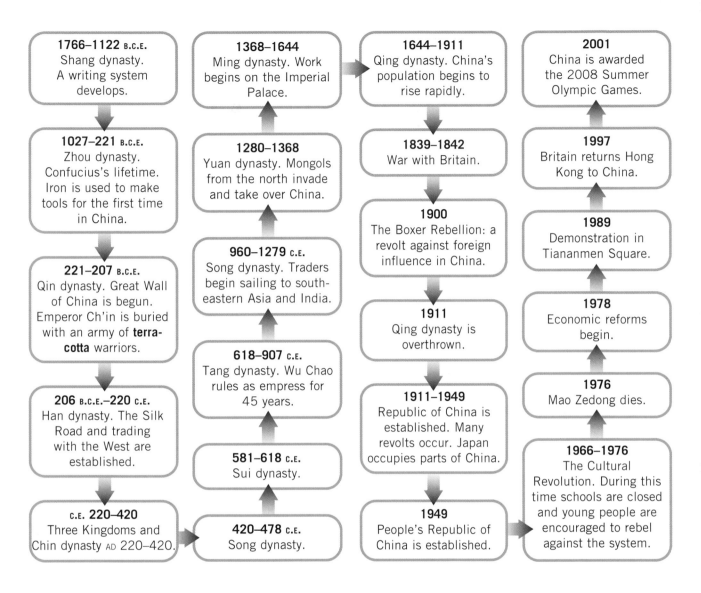

1766–1122 B.C.E.
Shang dynasty.
A writing system
develops.

1027–221 B.C.E.
Zhou dynasty.
Confucius's lifetime.
Iron is used to make
tools for the first time
in China.

221–207 B.C.E.
Qin dynasty. Great Wall
of China is begun.
Emperor Ch'in is buried
with an army of **terra-
cotta** warriors.

206 B.C.E.–220 C.E.
Han dynasty. The Silk
Road and trading
with the West are
established.

C.E. 220–420
Three Kingdoms and
Chin dynasty AD 220–420.

1368–1644
Ming dynasty. Work
begins on the Imperial
Palace.

1280–1368
Yuan dynasty. Mongols
from the north invade
and take over China.

960–1279 C.E.
Song dynasty. Traders
begin sailing to south-
eastern Asia and India.

618–907 C.E.
Tang dynasty. Wu Chao
rules as empress for
45 years.

581–618 C.E.
Sui dynasty.

420–478 C.E.
Song dynasty.

1644–1911
Qing dynasty. China's
population begins to
rise rapidly.

1839–1842
War with Britain.

1900
The Boxer Rebellion: a
revolt against foreign
influence in China.

1911
Qing dynasty is
overthrown.

1911–1949
Republic of China is
established. Many
revolts occur. Japan
occupies parts of China.

1949
People's Republic of
China is established.

2001
China is awarded
the 2008 Summer
Olympic Games.

1997
Britain returns Hong
Kong to China.

1989
Demonstration in
Tiananmen Square.

1978
Economic reforms
begin.

1976
Mao Zedong dies.

1966–1976
The Cultural
Revolution. During this
time schools are closed
and young people are
encouraged to rebel
against the system.

China: Facts & Figures

The red in China's flag symbolizes revolution. The large star represents the ruling Communist Party and the smaller stars represent the Chinese people.

People and Places

- Population: 1.3 billion
- Average life expectancy: men – 71; women – 74
- In China, a person's last name is followed by their first name, so Mao Zedong is Mr. Mao not Mr. Zedong.
- The lowest point in China is the Turpan Pendi basin, in the northwest. It is 505 feet (154 meters) below sea level.

Technology Boom

- There are more cell phones in China than land lines (269 million cell phones and 263 million land lines in 2003).
- In the next five years it is estimated that 178 million more people will buy a computer.

China's Industry

- Major crops: rice, potatoes, sorghum, peanuts.
- Natural resources: coal, iron ore, crude oil, mercury, tin.
- Major industries: iron, steel, coal.
- The world's biggest shoe factory is in Guangdong province and employs 80,000 people.

Glossary

amphibian animal, such as a frog, that lives both in water and on land

ancestor person from whom you are descended

arable land that is suitable for growing crops

autonomous being separate or able to govern a region independently

climate regular pattern of weather in an area

Communist person who follows a political belief system that calls for a classless society, where nobody owns anything and resources belong to a community

contour curved shape

drought temporary shortage of water

dynasty series of rulers from the same family

ethnic group people with the same culture or nationality

extinction no longer existing

fertile land that is good for growing crops

floodplain area that floods when river water rises

funding money given to an organization for a particular purpose

growing season period when it is warm enough for crops to grow

gunpowder explosive powder used to shoot bullets from guns

hydroelectric electricity created by moving water

limestone rock created from the remains of sea animals

Mandarin official language of China

manufacturing making things from raw materials

martial art type of unarmed self-defense, often practiced as a sport

meditating method of relaxing and concentrating to calm the mind and body

metro rail system in an urban area

missionary person who goes to other countries to do religious work

municipality main city in China that has the same status as a province

peasant poor person who lived and worked off the land

plateau area of high, flat land

port where ships load and unload cargo

preserved kept from decaying or falling down

province region that has its own local government

reform change made by the government to improve the country

rural relating to the countryside

self-sufficient able to produce enough food for the population

silt fine particles of sand and rock carried and then deposited by a river

terrace step or ledge cut into a hillside

terra-cotta type of clay

terrain area of land

terrestrial vertebrate animal that has a backbone and lives on land

tropical anything to do with the region either side of the Equator

turbine engine powered by water

typhoon storm with very strong winds

urban relating to a city or built-up area

Index